Swedenborg
Bifrons

By
Helena P. Blavatsky

Copyright © 2022 Lamp of Trismegistus. All rights reserved. No part of this publication may be reproduced or transmitted in any form or by any means, electronic or mechanical, including photocopying, recording, or by any information storage and retrieval system, without permission in writing from Lamp of Trismegistus. Reviewers may quote brief passages.

ISBN: 978-1-63118-604-2

Esoteric Classics

Other Books in this Series and Related Titles

Aurora of the Philosophers by Paracelsus (978-1-63118-507-6)

Rosicrucian Rules, Secret Signs, Codes and Symbols by various (978-1-63118-488-8)

On the Philadelphian Gold by Philochrysus & Philadelphus (978-1-63118-511-3)

Paracelsus, the Four Elements and Their Spirits by M P Hall (978-1-63118-400-0)

The Stone of the Philosophers by A E Waite (978-1-63118-509-0)

Clairvoyance and Psychic Abilities by A Besant &c (978-1-63118-403-1)

The Rosicrucian Chemical Marriage by Christian Rosenkreuz (978-1-63118-458-1)

The Alchemical Catechism of Paracelsus by Paracelsus (978-1-63118-513-7)

Alchemy in the Nineteenth Century by Helena P. Blavatsky (978-1-63118-446-8)

Rosicrucians and Speculative Masonry in the Seventeenth Century (978-1-63118-489-5)

Qabbalistic Teachings and the Tree of Life by M P Hall (978-1-63118-482-6)

The Sepher Yetzirah and the Qabalah by M P Hall (978-1-63118-481-9)

The Devil in Love by Jacques Cazotte (978–1–63118–499–4)

Fortune-Telling with Dice by Astra Cielo (978-1-63118-466-6)

History, Analysis and Secret Tradition of the Tarot by Hall &c (978-1-63118-445-1)

Crystal Vision Through Crystal Gazing by Frater Achad (978-1-63118-455-0)

The Golden Verses of Pythagoras: Five Translations (978-1-63118-479-6)

Arcane Formulas or Mental Alchemy by W W Atkinson (978-1-63118-459-8)

The Machinery of the Mind by Dion Fortune (978-1-63118-451-2)

The A E Waite Reader: A Selection of Occult Essays (978-1-63118-515-1)

The Leadbeater Reader: A Selection of Occult Essays (978-1-63118-483-3)

Audio versions are also available on Audible, Amazon and Apple

Other Books in this Series and Related Titles

Practical Use of Psychic Powers by C W Leadbeater (978-1-63118-603-5)

Using White & Black Magic by C W Leadbeater (978-1-63118-602-8)

Jesus, the Last Great Initiate by Edouard Schure (978-1-63118-599-1)

Mysterious Wonders of Antiquity by Manly P Hall (978-1-63118-598-4)

Ancient Mysteries and Secret Societies by Manly P Hall (978–1–63118–597–7)

The Zodiac and Its Signs by Manly P Hall (978–1–63118–596–0)

Life and Teachings of Hermes Trismegistus by Manly P Hall (978–1–63118–595–3)

The Secrets of Doctor Taverner by Dion Fortune (978–1–63118–594–6)

Vegetarianism, Theosophy & Occultism by Leadbeater &c (978–1–63118–593–9)

Applied Theosophy by Henry S Olcott (978–1–63118–592–2)

Higher Consciousness by C W Leadbeater (978–1–63118–591–5)

Theories About Reincarnation and Spirits by H P Blavatsky (978–1–63118–590–8)

The Use and Power of Thought by C W Leadbeater (978–1–63118–589–2)

Commentary on the Pymander by G R S Mead (978–1–63118–588–5)

Hypnotism and Mesmerism by Annie Besant (978–1–63118–587–8)

Spirits of Various Kinds by Helena P Blavatsky (978–1–63118–586–1)

The Hidden Language of Symbolism by Annie Besant (978–1–63118–585–4)

Eastern Magic & Western Spiritualism by Henry S Olcott (978–1–63118–584–7)

Spiritual Progress and Practical Occultism by H P Blavatsky (978–1–63118–583–0)

Memory and Consciousness by Besant & Blavatsky (978–1–63118–582–3)

The Origin of Evil by Helena P Blavatsky (978–1–63118–581–6)

Audio versions are also available on Audible, Amazon and Apple

Table of Contents

Introduction...7

Swedenborg Bifrons...9

The Deity...19

The Hells...21

Christians and Gentiles...23

Transmigration...27

INTRODUCTION

The word "esoteric" can be difficult to define. Esotericism in general can be seen less as a system of beliefs and more as a category, which encompasses numerous, different systems of beliefs. It's a bit of juxtaposition, since the word "esoteric" indicates something that few people know about, while the term itself broadly covers numerous philosophies, practices, areas of study and belief systems.

In a greater sense, Esotericism acts as a storehouse for secret knowledge, which is often considered ancient (by *tradition, if not by fact*), passed down from generation to generation, in private. At various times in history, simply possessing the knowledge of some of these subjects, was considered illegal and a jailable offence, if discovered. This usually included such general topics as Alchemy, Pharmacology, Qabalah, Hermeticism, Occultism, Ceremonial Magic, Astrology, Divination, Rosicrucianism and so on. Collectively, these areas of study were often referred to as the esoteric sciences.

Sometimes, the outer garment of a subject isn't esoteric, while what is hidden beneath it, is. As an example, Freemasonry isn't necessarily esoteric by nature (at *least not anymore*), but certain signs, passwords and handshakes given to the candidate during their initiation, are in fact, esoteric, in the sense that they are hidden from the general public.

Today, in the twenty-first century, such topics are readily available at bookstores across the country, and numerous main-steam publishers offer beginners guides and coffee-table volumes on many of these subjects, intended for mass appeal. Books like *"The Secret"* have turned previously arcane topics into household knowledge. All that being the case, however, it isn't to say that there still aren't buried secrets to uncover, ancient wisdom being ignored and forgotten mysteries to be explored. In fact, it is often that we are only able to further our own studies by standing on the shoulders of these disappearing giants.

Lamp of Trismegistus is doing its part to help preserve humanity's esoteric history by making some of these classics available to those students who are seeking to unearth the knowledge of these ancient colossi.

So, be sure to check other titles from our *Esoteric Classics* series, as well as our *Occult Fiction, Theosophical Classics, Foundations of Freemasonry Series, Supernatural Fiction, Paranormal Research Series, Studies in Buddhism* and our *Christian Apocrypha Series.* You can also download the audio versions of most of these titles from Amazon, Apple or Audible, for learning on the go.

SWEDENBORG BIFRONS

OR

SWEDENBORG, THE NEW CHURCH SECT, AND THE THEOSOPHICAL SOCIETY

A Critique by a Fellow of the Theosophical Society[1]

The word Bifrons should not here be taken in an ill-sense —T.P.S.

"*Errors cease first to be dangerous when they can be confuted. When known as very errors, they sink into the Abyss of Oblivion, and Truth alone hovers over the Immeasurable Space of the Centuries*". — HELVETIUS.

SWEDENBORG died in 1772, in the 85th year of his age. He had in his life-time quietly, and at his own expense, published and gratuitously distributed his theosophic writings. In time some of these fell into the hands of an English printer, named Hindmarsh, who, in conjunction with a few friends that had like himself become interested in them, formed a "Theosophical Society" for the study, translation, and publication of them. This happened about twelve years after Swedenborg's decease. But Mr. Hindmarsh, and some of his friends, became after a while dissatisfied with the plain, democratic fare of the "Theosophical Society", and began to lust after the flesh-pots of Ritualism. Well, the society dismembered. Whereupon Mr. Hindmarsh and his sympathisers prepared a creed and a liturgy (after the pattern of the Church of England), ordained

---

[1] Often cited as Madame Blavatsky, who anonymously authored similar articles in the same publication.

two of their own number (to baptise the rest and administer bread and wine to them) and coolly proclaimed the Second Advent of Jesus of Nazareth and the establishment of a new church by him (*sic.*) through his servant Emanuel Swedenborg! As time passed, the "New Church" grew a little, though with sighs, struggles, and throes; for divers souls with divers ideas began to enter the new fold, and, worse than this, began to read the Swedenborgian books with an effect different from that of the Hindmarshians; for they began seriously to question the legitimacy of the Hindmarshian interpretation of them. And so it came to pass that parties arose, and multiplied, that wordy and hot discussions ensued, and that the "Lord's New Church" began to quake!

What caused the quaking?

This: some read in the Swedenborgian books that Jesus was an avatar of Jehovah; others, that he was a myth, or a symbol of the descent of the Divine Principle in man into matter, its suffering and death in it, and its final resurrection out of it into oneness with the Absolute Existence; some read in them that the New Church vaticinated by Swedenborg is the ecclesiastical, Hindinarshian organization; others, that is it a regenerate state of the soul; some read that Jesus rose with his physical body into heaven; others, that this body saw corruption in the sepulchre; and some read that to obtain salvation it is essential for every "receiver" of Swedenborg's teachings to withdraw from the upas-like atmosphere of the "Old Church" (the Greek, Romish, and Protestant sects) and by re-baptism to enter the "New Church"; others read that salvation may be obtained within any of the sects of the *Protestant* church!

Although thus from the outset bearing within itself the seeds of disintegration, in the shape of parties, "at daggers drawing one with another", the Hindinarshian sect has like a sloth crept down the century, neither growing much numerically nor diminishing; and has meanwhile, under the cover of Swedenborg's name, brazenly proclaimed itself the sole possessor of the Divine Truth — the only bride and wife of the Lamb.

Well, hundreds of Christian sects have done so, do it, and will do it: and were it not that I regarded Swedenborg, in spite of his many contradictions, as a true Theosophist, and loved to see him placed before the world in a true light, I would verily not take up my pen against the sophomorical claims of the Hindmarshian sect ; because I care in reality as little for these as for those of any other sect.

The knowledge touching Swedenborg in the possession of the public has hitherto come almost exclusively through this sect: no matter whether we take up a pamphlet or an Encyclopedia Britannica, we find the information therein given to be from this source, and so, one-sided and untrustworthy. It ever represents Swedenborg's teaching as altogether Christian; either drawn straight out of the Bible by him, or given orally to him by Jesus in person. All biographies of Swedenborg in existence (save a brief one by Philangi Dàsa) are, therefore, to use a Carlylean phrase, "wretched puckeries and botcheries", representing him either in the halo of a Genevan Calvinist or a New England Puritan: thus neither as a god, an angel, or a rational man, but as a simpering Pharisee. Falsehoods, nay, lies have thus far been liberally used in the production of some of these biographies. I say this with a full knowledge of the meaning of what I say. If facts have happened to please the fancy and narrow-mindedness of the biographers, they have been freely published and generally grossly magnified; if not, they have been suppressed. I admit that the suppression of certain dreams in Swedenborg's private diary has been judicious. I myself would have suppressed them. They were Swedenborg's private property, and were not intended for the irrationally vulgar, either within or without the "New Church" sect. They are useful in the hands of a philosopher, but not so in the hands of a fool — religious or irreligious. But what I do not justify is the suppression of his theosophic teachings — as, with great sedulity and for jesuitic purposes, has hitherto been the case. I would not give an ace for all the "New Church" literature afloat — whether published in the organs of the sect or in the Encyclopedias— touching Swedenborg's teachings. I am thoroughly familiar with all that has been published both in Europe and in America with regard to them; and I do not hesitate to say that, with three exceptions, which I shall presently mention, I would not, for the trouble of carting it home, accept it as a gift. Please understand me: I have reference solely to doctrinal statements and inferences, not to mere historical facts.

The outcome of this jesuitical one-sidedness on the part of the Christian students of Swedenborg was very well illustrated in the case of Rao Bahadur Dadoba Pandurung, a Hindu, and, if I mistake not, a member of the Theosophical Society, who studied some of our author's writings in the light of the Hindmarshian sect, and wrote a book entitled, "A Hindu Gentleman's Reflections respecting the Works of Swedenborg and the Doctrines of the New Jerusalem Church". For, had a preacher of the sect written it, it could not have been more orthodox (and misleading) than it is. Not that Pandurung intended it to be so — far from it:— but he himself had been misled. Had he read the works of students of Swedenborg like Tulk, James, and Dàsa, I am confident he would not have written it; for he was an intelligent man. The same may be said of a series of articles written by Dr. H. C. Vatterling and published in *The Theosophist*, headed, "Studies in Swedenborg". These represent the teachings of our good Swede as seen through the spectacles of the "New Church" sect. Indeed, so pleasing were they to that sect that its most orthodox organ, the *New Church Life*, noticed them favourably; though to notice anything favourably that is published in a journal so "godless" as *The Theosophist*, is contrary to its policy. Now, the difference between looking at Swedenborg's teachings through the spectacles of the "New Church" sect, and those of a Tulk, a James, or a Dàsa, is the same as looking at the biblical teachings through the spectacles of a Wesley and those of a Gerald Massey or a Colenso.

The first prominent dissenter from the Hindmarshian sect was the late Charles Augustus Tulk, an Englishman and Member of Parliament. In a work entitled "Spiritual Christianity" he proves, after a lengthy, critical, and exhaustive study of Swedenborg, that he did not at heart believe in the personal god of the "New Church" creed, but in an impersonal, Divine Principle; nor in a personal Jesus, but in a subjective Christ-principle; nor in an ecclesiastical church organization, but in a life of good, unselfish use to humanity.

The second prominent dissenter was the late Henry James (sr.), an American literatus of great acumen, who wrote several books to show that the "secret of Swedenborg" is a *subjectiveness* of heaven and of all things Divine, and not, as the thoughtless suppose, an *objectiveness* of them. In other words, God, Christ, heaven, hell, and the church are, each and all, according to Swedenborg, entities and states of the Human soul: — *subjective*, therefore, and not *objective*. James treats with Carlylean scorn and mordacity the objective "New Church" and its aperies as most pernicious and death-doing interpretations of Swedenborg.

The third prominent dissenter is Philangi Dàsa; who has written a work entitled "Swedenborg the Buddhist"; in which he proves, from Swedenborg, not only all that Tulk and James have proved, but also, in addition, that Swedenborg, very far from being a sound Christian, and in communication with a personal Jesus, was a very sound Pagan, and in communication (by occult means) with Buddhist Yogis and Arhats and their disciples. This writer has the advantage of his precursors, Tulk and James, in this respect, that he has had the benefit of works of scholars like Koeppen, Lassen, Bournouf, Rhys-Davids, Max Müller, Beale, and many others; not to speak of the priceless works published by the Theosophical Society. Had these existed in Tulk's day, I am confident the "New Church" sect would not now exist. But Europe was then in belluine ignorance with regard to the archaic religions and philosophies of Asia. This was well illustrated when Swedenborg, upon the publication of his theosophical writings, in England and Holland, sent copies of them to Swedish Prelates and friends. The majority merely glanced at them, and then shelved them; but a few read them, grew angry and began to vociferate about atheistic, Mohammedan innovations ! and actually took steps to have a writ *de lunatico inquirendo* issued. But Swedenborg's influential position, as well as his relationship by birth and marriage to both ecclesiastical and political dignitaries, frustrated it. Mohammedan innovations ! The priests of that day were familiar with the triplet religious sisters of the Occident — Judaism, Christianism, and Mohammedanism; but not with those of the Orient,—Buddhism, Brahmanism, and Zoroastrianism. It was plain to them, notwithstanding the thick, Christian bronze-lacquer, with which Swedenborg has overlaid his "new Christian religion", that there was, in Hamlet's words, "something rotten in the state of Denmark", and what could this be but atheism and Mohammedanism ! These charges Swedenborg declared to be "wicked lies, invented by craft, and two deadly stigmas, designed to avert and deter the minds of men from the holy worship of the Lord" (T.137) [The abbreviated titles of Swedenborg's works referred to in these pages are as follows: A Arcana Coelestia. E Apocalypse Explained. R. Apocalypse Revealed. B Brief Exposition. M. Conjugal Love. Coro. Coronis. W. Divine Love and Wisdom. P. Divine Providence. I. Intercourse between Soul and Body. J. Last Judgment. D. Diary. S. Sacred Scriptures. T. True Christian Religion. W.L. Worship and Love of God. Doc. Documents];—the "Lord", as presented in his writings, of course !

The spread of the "New Church" sect has almost exclusively been confined to England and the United States of America, the two countries in the West, in which the critical study of religious subjects is as yet in its infancy. On the Continent, notwithstanding strong pecuniary support from these countries, it has made no headway. But, as the object of this critique is not the mere history of the Hindmarshian sect, I shall forbear to go into details — to give the causes of this non-success, and to enumerate the many "heresies" and bitter fights, with which the sect, owing to the miscellaneous, strange, and contradictory teachings of Swedenborg, has been infested and torn, — and content myself with the relation of the following extraordinary fact:

Swedenborg has, in the sect, been held as *the* authority in all spiritual matters. The phrase, "Swedenborg says so", has ever been sufficient to suppress (loud) thought, stop reason, and make honest inquiry synonymous with impiety and profanation; in one word, it has ever been sufficient to freeze or fossilize the mind in the Hindmarshian mould. The infallibility of Swedenborg has therefore always been tacitly admitted. But it fell to the lot of a young countryman of Swedenborg, a bold, uncompromising and fanatical preacher of the sect in America, openly to assert the infallibility-dogma. This assertion created, however, at the time no sensation, for his hearers had already in private been prepared for it. The new dogma spread, and became in a short time, within the party to which he belonged, a shibboleth of "New Church" orthodoxy. Let us see if I misrepresent: *The New Church Messenger* (New York) for December 21, 1887, contains the following paragraph: "All New Church papers accept the writings of the New Church (*i.e.* of Swedenborg) as a divine revelation. *The New Church Life* goes a step further and says: consequently, they are an *infallible divine authority*. To dispute the one proposition is to dispute both".

In view of the fact that we have the original writings of Swedenborg before us, and also in view of the fact that our "New Church" brethren do not inhabit Patagonia, but lands in which scholarship and reason are coming into ascendency, this is certainly an extraordinary claim. The same claim made by Loyola's Black Militia for the Bishop of Rome is absurd and impudent enough, but as it rests upon tradition, it does not in these respects, approach this, made by Hindmarsh's Foolish Militia for Swedenborg.

There is one subject upon which all the parties of the sect are agreed; namely this, that Swedenborg has for the first time revealed the genuine, inner meaning of the Bible, and that this revelation, founded upon his (?) "science of correspondence" will stand any crucial test that may be applied to it. Now, it behoves us not to reject this claim, but to test it; for which purpose let us go straight to the writings of our "divine" revelator, to see how he "infallibly" draws forth the hidden meaning of the Bible:

"And they that are with Him are called, and chosen, and faithful". — Revelation, xvii. 14.	
The 'Called (says Swedenborg) means those that are in the *highest* form of love	The 'Called' (says Swedenborg) means those that are the *lowest* form of love.
The 'Faithful" means those that are in the *lowest* form of love – A.E. 1074	The 'Faithful' means those that are the *highest* form of love – A.R 744
The Apostolic Word has *not* an internal sense – A. 10325	The Apostolic Word *has* an internal sense. The internal sense of Acts ii 1 – 4 is given in A.E. 455
In A.R. 95 he rejects the phrase," yet thou art rich" (Rev ii 9) because it is "omitted in some manuscripts".	In A.E. 118 this phrase is "'divine" and has an internal sense; which is there given

I could easily fill page upon page with specimens like these of the "internal sense" of the Bible, now "infallibly" and for the first time drawn forth from it by Swedenborg; but, *cui bono* ?

The orthodox members of the Hindmarshian sect have for many years past discussed the advisability of translating the Bible in the light afforded by Swedenborg; that is to say, of translating his Latin translation into English; and, where he has not translated the Hebrew, of translating it in the light of the "Lord's New Church". And, if I mistake not, the work has been informally begun. King James' version will not do; for in hundreds of instances it does not agree with Swedenborg; nor will Queen Victoria's; being a "sacrilegious mangling" of the "infallible" Hebrew edition of Everard van der Hooght! But Swedenborg did not translate as much of the Hebrew of Van der Hooght's edition into Latin, as his uncritical students imagine. He copied, as a rule, the Latin of Sebastian Schmidt.

The "New Church" sect claims that Swedenborg, with the personal help of Jesus, has drawn forth *the* spiritual meaning of the Bible; and it stands therefore to reason that his understanding and rendering of the sacred volume must be infallible; for no one can, out of the fallible, draw forth anything infallible. Let us therefore look at Swedenborg as a translator:

And the court that is *without* (extra) the temple, cast out, and measure it not – Rev. xi 2) in A.R.	And the court that is *within* (intra) the temple, cast out, and measure it not – A. 730
They made them (the idols) to bow themselves down to the moles and the *wasps* (vespis). Is. ii 20, 21, in A. 9424	They made them to bow themselves down to the moles and *bats* (vespertilionibus) — A. 8932; 10582. E. 410
May the blessing of thy father prevail above the blessings of my parents; may they be upon the head of Joseph and upon the crown of the *bed* (lectus) of his brethren. – Gen xlix 26, in E 163	The blessings of thy father will prevail over the blessing of my sires, even to the longing desires of the hills of an age they will be for the head of Joseph, and for the crown of the head of the *Nazariteship* (Naziraei) of his brethren, – A. 3969

I could also in this respect fill page upon page with specimens like these, but it would only weary the reader. We have now had a glimpse of Swedenborg as an expositor and translator of the Bible; it remains to get a glimpse of him as a teacher of doctrine. To this end, and to be as brief as possible, let me take up, say, four different subjects: (1) the Deity, (2) the Hells, (3) Christians and Gentiles, and (4) Transmigration.

THE DEITY

SWEDENBORG THE CHRISTIAN: We must worship Jehovah, the father of God-Messiah, our Saviour (D. 169); we must also worship his son, Jesus, as a mediator between him and ourselves (D. 408; 526). If we do not believe in the Son we must inevitably be damned to hell (D. 857); for the Son alone has on the cross been made justice for us all (D. 273); having offered himself a sacrifice for the sins of the whole world, (T. 727) when the Omnipotent was about to punish the race because of sin (W. L. 78). As to the nature of the union of the Son and his Father, it is not for us to try to penetrate this mystery (D. 1595). He that sees the Son, the intercessor between the Father and the human race, sees the Father himself. This is sufficient to know. It is useless and impious to go deeper into mystery (D. 1601). For my own part, I desire always to have my crucified Saviour before my eyes, because his blood and merit help me (Doc. V. ii. p. 178, 186). Every one that desires to be truly a Christian, and desires to be saved by Christ, must believe that Jesus is the Son of the Living God (T. 342); and that the name of Jesus is so holy that it cannot be named by any devil in hell (T. 297).

SWEDENBORG THE THEOSOPHIST: It is said that it is useless and impious to try to enter into the mysteries of faith. Do not believe it. For, "*it is now lawful to enter intellectually into the mysteries of faith*" (T. 508). The Divine Life is *not* a person (W. 71), not a he or a she, a father or a son. It is a principle, which, though it pervades all space, is itself spaceless; and though it pervades all time, is itself timeless (W. 7 ; T. 30). The worlds, visible and invisible, supernal and infernal, spiritual and material; and all beings, divine and undivine, human and animal, have come forth from it (T. 32; 43; 44). And all that has come forth from it is eternal; that is, divine in itself (E. 1130), and returns in the end to it (E. 1129). It is correct to say that we are *in* the Divine Life (though we are not conscious of it), and that everything is full of it (W. L. 58; 98). The personal gods of the priests are but the anthropomorphic projections of their own mind. The only personal god I have seen was a reflection, outside me, of the personal god (the Sixth-Seventh principle) inside me (H. 39; 79; 147; 435) For all good men see inwardly, in themselves, their Divine Being (E. 151). It is useless to trouble oneself about the gods of books and men: for *Life* and *Nature* are the causes of all entities and things (I. 10, II), and are all-sufficient! As to the statement that the name of Jesus cannot be uttered in hell, this is a mistake: I have heard it uttered there (D. 228). And as to the statement that to be saved one has to believe in Jesus, this is another mistake: for the faith of the Gentiles saves them (T. 107).

THE HELLS

SWEDENBORG THE CHRISTIAN: God has given to man rationality and liberty to choose between good and evil. And he has also predestined him for heaven. Therefore, if he goes to hell he goes thither from deliberate choice (E. 802); and stays there eternally (E. 383). The man that does not purge himself of inherited and actual evils has hell in him, and comes after death in hell, and remains there eternally (E. 1164). Self-love and worldly love are the two great banes which cause man to cast himself into eternal punishment in hell (E. 837). You have doubtless heard the pernicious falsehood that God can save whomsoever he pleases, and that he will in the end save all, even those in hell. But I solemnly assure you that, a soul once in hell remains there everlastingly (H. 521 — 7, E. 745, A. 967). For, as the tree falls so it lies. Emendation after death is not possible (D. 4037 — 8, H. 508). I would caution you not to think that infants and little children — even of Pagan parentage — are permitted to go to hell, for the lord takes all that die in infancy and childhood to himself (H. 329)

SWEDENBORG THE THEOSOPHIST: Man, it is said, was predestined for heaven, and if he goes to hell it is his own fault. Can anyone predestined for a state escape it ? All this twaddle is the outcome of a belief in a personal god. The evil done here bears in its bosom its own punishment (D. 2438). But this punishment is even proportionate to the evil, or rather to the selfish *motive* that prompted it. As the effect of a particular evil cannot, any more than the evil itself, be everlasting, so neither can the punishment. I have been taught that to every man an opportunity is given after death (in a future incarnation) to amend his life, if possible (P. 328). A man suffers until the selfishness in him is subjugated (D, 1742); that is, until it exhausts itself. Otherwise he would suffer endlessly (D. 2709;

4596); which would be useless and contrary to the Law of Mercy. Those that hereafter come into the various hellish states are by degrees taken out of them and elevated into heavenly (D. 1741). Wherefore, damnation is at last taken away (D. 2583), I have seen many of the damned raised out of hell and torments into heaven, where they now live (D. 228). It would indeed be foolish to suppose that anyone would be permitted to be punished in hell everlastingly for the sins of one so short life as this. The end of all punishment in view is reformation. But eternal punishment could have no such end in view, and would therefore be useless (D. 3489). The Divine Law is, that nothing is ever without a use (D. 3144). When the effect of man's selfishness; of his self love and worldly love, has exhausted itself, the Divine Principle intervenes and liberates him out of hell (D. 2826). When I speak of hell, I do not, of course, have in mind an *objective* hell, but a *subjective*: a low, selfish state of the soul, with its train of sufferings.

CHRISTIANS AND GENTILES

SWEDENBORG THE CHRISTIAN: A Christian is one that knows the Lord (Jesus), has the Word (the Bible), and belongs to the (Protestant) Church: and he, more than anyone that is not a Christian, has the capacity of being regenerated, or becoming spiritual (M. 339). In other words, to attain to salvation it is not merely necessary to be good naturally (as many of the Gentiles are), one has to be good spiritually. Now spiritual goodness has its source only in the truths of the Christian faith; and it is this goodness that confers eternal life (A. 8772). It is Christian goodness that makes heaven; nothing else (A. 7197). I do not say that a Gentile may not be saved; he may indeed, if only he has worshipped a god under a human form (an anthropomorphic god), and has lived a good life. This will admit him into the company of Christians in heaven (J. 51). But then, no matter how good a Gentile may be, he cannot be, as it were, of the heart or of the very centre of heaven; for this is possible only to a Christian. When I say *Christian*, I do not, of course, mean a Papist (for the Papists are not Christians; — N. 8), but I mean a Protestant (S. 105).

You seem to wonder that the Christians are in the very centre of heaven, and nearest the Lord (Jesus); but from personal observation I assure you that this is a fact (T. 678, D. 5240). And the English Christians, because of their exalted intelligence, form the very cream of heaven (T. 807). The Lord Jesus is the Central Life of the Universe, and those that worship him alone are after death drawn to him. A man, born in the Christian world, who does not believe in Jesus, is never admitted into heaven, nor are his prayers heard (T. 108). Nay, more than this, a man that does not in the world live a Christian life cannot after death even name Jesus (P. 262). I have just said that the Papists are not Christians; let me add that neither are those Christians who deny the holiness of the Word (Bible) .— P. 256. I think it expedient to tell you, by all means to have your children baptized very early into the Christian faith; for, while an infant remains unbaptized, some straggling Mohammedan or Pagan spirit may see him, and by occult means, unknown to you, alienate him from Christianity (T. 678). Therefore, let him be baptized, and let him receive the sign of the cross upon his forehead and breast (T. 682). When he reaches manhood, and feels himself burdened with sins, it will do him good to confess them to a priest and receive absolution (T. 539). Let me call your attention to this, that a pure marriage-love can exist only between one Christian man and one Christian woman (M. 337). That is to say, the Christian marriage principle alone is chaste, because it is spiritual (M. 142; 339). And because it is chaste and spiritual it is the very store-house of the Christian religion (M. 457). Concubinage, *without a really serious reason*, closes heaven against man, and the angels do not number him among the Christians (M. 464). I might add that the Lord (Jesus), the only God of heaven and earth, has appeared to me *in person*, and has, through me, revealed the mysteries of the Word (Bible), of heaven, of hell, and of the earth, and has so made his promised Second Advent. He has also, through me, established a New Christian Church, which will last eternally, and so be the crown of all the churches that have existed (Coro. LIX.); and he has moreover formed a new heaven into which only Christians will be admitted (R. 876).

SWEDENBORG THE THEOSOPHIST: The idea of three gods has prevailed among the Christians since the establishment of their schismatic and heretical church (H. 2. B. 63. P. 262. T. 378); and this idea, including the Vicarious Atonement, has led to all manner of abominations. The Christians are at heart idolaters and atheists (A. 2605); and the angels say that they are spiritually insane (T. 134); men-beasts and prating parrots (T. 160; 391); and that they believe nothing but what their natural senses tell them. Thus they are worshippers of Nature (A. 5572; 5639; 6876). They openly profess to believe in Jesus and in the Bible, but at heart they deny both, and, have contempt for them (A. 3472-9-89). They have no spiritual illumination, and are not affected by the truth. Of true goodness they are ignorant, and also of a life hereafter. They go to church for selfish and worldly reasons, and care not a whit whether the doctrine taught be true or false (A. 9409). Not a single one among them knows what heavenly joy is (M. 2); nor what conscience is (T. 666). And nowhere in the world do we find a more detestable life than in Christendom (A. 916). Hence it is that the doctrine of charity is much more easily embraced by the Gentiles than by the Christians (A. 932; 4190; 2284); for the former are not so befogged spiritually as the latter. When we enter the Spiritual World, we find that the worst souls there are from those that profess themselves Christians (D. 480). They are full of hatred and hypocrisy (A. 1032; 1886. D. 3595; 3613; 5539; 480). Think scarcely of anything but greatness, power and profanity (A. 2122); have no regard for the neighbour (especially if he be a Gentile), and are, above all in the world, obscene, adulterous, and domineering (A. 2752 - 4 ; 8772). *The Christians are in fact so corrupt that the Lord has betaken himself to the Gentiles* (D. 5807) and the angels have slender hopes of the Christians (J. 74). When the Gentiles are instructed in spiritual matters, they are in a clearer, more interior, perception or intuition, than the Christians (A. 9256); and many more of them are saved (A. 2284). It may be truly said that, as far as the Christians are concerned, Intuition, or Perception, does not exist (A. 10737). The Gentiles wish well to the Christians, but they are in return despised, and, as much as possible, injured (A. 2590). The angels have told me that when the Gentiles die and enter the Spiritual world, they obtain in a single day rest, which, in the case of Christians, is scarcely obtained in thirty years (A. 2595; 298). The end of the Christian Church is now at hand; and the Lord's Kingdom will soon be found beyond the Christian world (A. 4535. D. 2567).

TRANSMIGRATION

SWEDENBORG THE CHRISTIAN: It is known that the ancient Gentiles believed that the Soul pre-existed: that it was created in the beginning of the World, and that afterwards it entered into conjunction with the Body. Well, this was a delusion, the outcome of intercourse with lying spirits (T.). I have again and again instructed spirits, who have imagined that their Soul has always existed, that this is a wicked delusion (D. 1673; 2180½ *et al*). The Soul of every man is conceived by his father. Conception is, therefore, a purely masculine function. A woman cannot conceive a Soul (T. 110). The Creator inserts the elements of the Soul of everyone into his father's Understanding, where they are formed by his Will into a Soul, which then descends into his Body, is there clothed with a certain covering from Nature, and is then transferred to his mother's womb to receive a gross Body. There is, therefore, in everyone a graft or offset of his father's Soul in its fulness (T. 103; 112; 171; 584). The reason why the Soul is formed in the father is, because he is a rational being; which the mother, by herself, is not. The rationality and originality that a woman manifests are not hers, but some man or men's; for which cause the Ancients ordered that she should keep silent in the Church (A. 8994. M. 175) You wonder, I perceive, at the unlikeness of men or brothers: some being dull, gross, and bad; others, bright, refined, and good; and others again neither; and you ask, Why does the Creator make them so unlike? Now consider this: as the mould is, so is the thing moulded; or, as the father is, so is the son. The good done by a man is from the Creator; but the bad is in part from his father, or his father's paternal (not maternal) ancestors, and in part from himself (T. 521)

SWEDENBORG THE THEOSOPHIST: Man receives through his parents nothing but the Physical body (P. 330). His Soul is altogether independent of them. Man is, however, more than a duality of Soul and Body (T. 112); he is a trinity of Body, Mind, and Soul (D. 3185); and more than this, he is a quaternity of Body, Natural soul, Spiritual soul, and the Lord (D. 1313), M. 101); and still more than this, he is a septenary of Body, its Vitality, Sensual degree, Natural degree, Rational degree, Spiritual degree, and Divine degree (D. 3385; E. 726; 1056; 1127). With regard to the seven degrees let me state briefly that man receives the First and the Second from his parents and Nature; the Third and Fourth he creates for himself (D. 2794; 2837); the Fifth (the Human soul proper) is the result of his experiences; the Sixth is, or will be, so to say, the sweetness, the aroma, the fulness of the good and the true he has acquired (in his transmigrations), and the Seventh is the Divine Being; the Self-Infinite, or the God in man (E. 151; M. 135. W. L. 33). As to the statement that the doctrine of pre-existence is a spiritualistic and gentile delusion, depend upon it, the delusion is altogether on the side of those that make it. *"For man, as to all (omnes) his degrees, existed similarly before (ante) his nativity, as he exists afterward"* (D. 2591).

Reader: "Ex uno disce omnes!"

Had Swedenborg, like nearly all the founders of the various Christian sects, been a mere strainer at gnats and swallower of camels, he would, at this day, hardly be worth while our attention. For, since the foundation of the Theosophical Society, we have matters to think upon far more serious than the whims and ambitions of sectarists, bent upon hatching new dogmas out of the Bible, or out of their own brains: new dogmas of as little practical value as the old. But, after years of careful study of Swedenborg, I look upon him, notwithstanding his verbosities, wearisome reiterations, absurd claims, blunders, and exploded Christian dogmas, as one of the most useful allies pf the Theosophical Society. He, more than anyone else, has confirmed me in the belief that the Society has a glorious mission in the world. Swedenborg predicted the establishment of a New Church somewhere, outside Europe (A. 2986). Now, a Church in the true sense in which he uses this term, does not mean an ecclesiastical organization, like the Hindmarshian, Roman Catholic, or any other ; but a new, *rational* teaching — a new thought and a new life: *a worship of the Divine in Humanity, and a life of impersonal love toward humanity* (A. 3379; 4899). Has anything else been the real, underlying object of the Theosophical Society ?

I am well aware that Mr. Hindmarsh's "New Church" will stoutly, angrily, and sophistically object to this claim. But the claim of this sect, that Swedenborg with the help of Jesus of Nazareth, gave to the world a *new* revelation and established a new Church, has most effectively been exploded by Dàsa in "Swedenborg the Buddhist"; for he has therein brought the higher teachings of Buddhism, Brahmanism, Zoroastrianism, and even those of the ancient Goths and American Indians, as far as these are known, face to face with the theosophic teachings of Swedenborg; and has in this way demonstrated beyond cavil, that the "new" revelation is a very, very old revelation. Besides this, there is now publishing in America, a little monthly paper, *The Buddhist Ray*, "devoted to Buddhism in general, and to the *Buddhism in Swedenborg* in particular" — a fact upon which comment is altogether unnecessary !

Let us now look at the attitude of the "New Church" sect toward the Theosophical Society, and at that of the Society toward the sect. In 1882 the Society issued a pamphlet, entitled "Swedenborg and Theosophy", made up of two letters, the first from a Swedenborgian to a Theosophist; and the second, from the latter to the former. The first letter contains the usual, unfounded claims made by the "New Church" sect for Swedenborg; in brief, that the world is governed by a masculine, personal god; that, the Bible is his word; that we must look to Jesus of Nazareth for salvation; and to Swedenborg for an understanding of the Bible and a guidance to Jesus. The second letter is an able and temperate reply to these dogmas, and a very satisfactory confutation of them. It contains a statement anent Swedenborg which is as remarkable as it is true; this is namely: "There *are* (notice the tense) those amongst the Adepts (of Asia) who knew him (Swedenborg) well. Efforts were made to help him to clear his mind, and not altogether unsuccessfully; much of the truth he did bring back from other planes (to use his own phraseology) he owed to that assistance. No mystic with anything like Swedenborg's natural capacities ever dawns upon the world without persistent efforts being made by one or other of the Adepts to lead him to the absolute truth. But in his case (as in that of many others) this was impossible, owing to an ineradicable, erroneous fundamental conception which absolutely barred his ever rising to the perfect light, and always insensibly blurred and distorted this to his inner sight. This erroneous conception was the Western notion of an *omnipotent* PERSONAL God" (p. 12).

I agree with the writer: the obstacle in Swedenborg's way was an anthropomorphic deity. Still there is a large number of facts that go to prove that, though in some states of mind he believed in this deity, in others, he did not; as I have just shown from his writings.

Two or three years ago there appeared in London a book entitled the "Issues of Modern Thought", by a preacher of the Hindmarshian sect; the last chapter of which is devoted to a hypercriticism of the Theosophical Society, its work, and claims. The *Theosophist* published a review of it; with a few mild, good-naturedly ironic civilities, because of the presumptuous statement that the Mahatmas, or Adepts, that stand behind the Society are in league with the devils of the "Middle", or "Spiritual" hell! A writer in the *Buddhist Ray*, for May, 1888, asks pertinently the author, being that he is so confident, if he has visited the "Spiritual" hell and there seen the league.

The *New-Church Messenger* (New York) published last year a series of articles headed "Spiritualism, Theosophy, and Kindred Subjects", by another preacher of the sect. The statements therein made are but a stale reiteration of those made by the London preacher, with an additional display of childish assertion and ignorance with regard to the Theosophical Society. These articles have been re-published in pamphlet form and extensively circulated within and without the sect. For it has always been the desire of the Hindmarshians to appear well in the eyes of "Old Church" sects: to appear, not as a Mussalmanic, Spiritualistic, Theosophic, or Pagan organization, but as a genuinely Protestant Christian. Hence these "feeble-forcible" efforts.

The latest effort on their part, and the most "feeble-forcible", too, was made on the appearance of Dàsa's "Swedenborg the Buddhist". When the orthodox leaders of the sect had read it, it was plain to them that an honest criticism or review of it would be suicidal. And so they ordered a youth in their theological school in Philadelphia, to berate the founders of the Theosophical Society and to befoul the author. Why the former, who were altogether innocent in the matter, should be berated, is beyond my comprehension. The book is not a publication of the Society; nor are the founders even once mentioned in it. The attack upon them was, therefore, a piece of sheer deviltry, and a disgusting exhibition of the inward spirit of the "New Jerusalem Church". Well, the "review" (as the youth called it), appeared in the the *New-Church Life* for February, 1888, under the sensational heading, "A 'Theosophistical' Attack". When with many adjectives he thought he had sufficiently berated the founders of the Society, he sought his "New Church" spelling-book for a choice set of nouns wherewith to befoul the author; and boot-black, profaner, woman-hater, fool, caricature, and border-ruffian, were among those found, and with a score or more of exclamation-points, liberally used. There was not in the scurrility the faintest attempt to deal with the principles at issue; only personalities and scurrilities. So far did he forget himself that he attacked the "Studies in Swedenborg", which had appeared in the *Theosophist*, though these had a short time before, because of their Hindmarshian orthodoxy, received a complimentary notice in the *New-Church Life*.

The "New Church" sect has, since the founding of the Theosophical Society, publicly, and still more so privately, shown a great hatred of it and its teachings. Its journals never mention the Society without adding, "devoted to spiritism and sorcery", though they well know that Spiritism and Sorcery have proved its worst opponents. I have often heard surprise expressed at this. But to one that knows the inner life, the secret workings of the sect, which are carefully hidden from the world, the cause of this hatred is very plain. The leaders in the sect are only too well aware that all that glitters is not gold; that an unbiassed study of the teachings of Swedenborg, a study of them in the light of the Theosophical Society, will reveal the fact that, instead of being at the core genuinely Christian, newly sent down from heaven by Jesus of Nazareth, they are at the core genuinely theosophic, very, very old guests of this sublunary globe, to be found both in the archaic philosophies of Asia and in the publications of the Theosophical

Society; and this fact must therefore, by hook or by crook, be kept from the less knowing and less jesuitic members of the sect; and so they amuse them with shifts and personalities.

It would be to the credit of the "New Church" sect, if its leaders would cease to slander and misrepresent the Theosophical Society. And it would tend to the godly edification not only of its own members but also of the rest of the human family, if they would drop their present bones of contention; which are: (I) Whether the "New Church" worship of the dual god, Jehovah-Jesus, should be conducted by robed prelates, priests, and acolytes in imposing churches, or by plain preachers in simple meeting-houses. (2) Whether the blood of Jesus is properly represented by grape-juice or by wine. And (3) whether Swedenborg's work on "Scortatory Love" was written for the men of the "Lord's New Church", or for the men of the "Lord's Old Church": that is to say, whether or not the unmarried "New Church" man is ever justified in keeping a mistress, and the married man, a concubine. For I know that the *pros* and *cons*, these bones of contention, and the slanders, maledictions, and persecutions, in the name of the Lord and Swedenborg, growing out of them, have a most baneful effect upon the young — especially upon the young men; inasmuch as it fosters among them a sensuality and a materialism. It seems to me it would be wiser to keep before the young the Divine Truths that underlie the dogmas, sensualities, and formalities of the decaying Christian Church which impair the theosophic writings of Swedenborg. I believe this would be the policy of the Theosophical Society. And I am sure it would lead to the abandonment of formality for charity, drunkenness for soberness, and unchastity for chastity: and so help to upbuild the New Church vaticinated by Swedenborg and found nowhere but within the Theosophical Society.

It has hundreds of times been publicly stated, but upon what ground I do not know, that the real, invisible FOUNDERS of the Theosophical Society, the Mahatmas (Great Souls), have no existence: that They are figments of Madame H. P. Blavatsky, wherewith either to advertise her books, her "new religion", or herself (Ha!). Less sceptical persons of the Spiritualistic and Christian Swedenborgian creeds, believe in their existence; but explain that they are her "Spirit-Guides", or, "Devils of a Spiritual Hell". With these suppositions, theories, and statement in view, it is interesting and instructive to note the following statements made by Swedenborg, in the last century: First, that there exists a system of Spiritual Truth, of far more transcendent nature than any known in the world at this day; second, that it is in the hands of certain inhabitants of Central Asia (Buddhists); third, that it is inaccessible to the world at large, especially to Christians; fourth, that he, by occult means, and in the company of the possessors of it, visited Central Asia, and there got a glimpse of it; and fifth, that it should be sought for among the (Buddhist) inhabitants of China and Tartary. These statements were made at different times, and in different works of our author, between the years 1764-71. (See, M. 77. T. 279. Coro. 39. R. II. S. lOI. D. 6077).

Mr. T. L. Harris, the American Spiritualist and Mystic, has truly said: the World has had its ages of Gold, Silver, Copper, and Iron; the present is the Pulpit-age, the Age of Wind! When the preachers of the Hindmarshian sect, with Swedenborg in their pocket, rail at Madame Blavatsky (who, by the way, has never said a harsh or unjust word against them, and I would know!) and foam at the mouth about "her Mongolian hobgoblins" and "devils of a spiritual hell", there can be no doubt about the truth of Mr. Harris's statement. Heaven help all, of the "New Church" and of the "Old Church", who, instead of thinking and investigating for themselves, permit themselves to be carried away by "wind"!

I must tell the reader that there are many students of Swedenborg who are not members of the sect; who have a great contempt for it, and oftentimes a great hatred of it; as may be seen in their organ, the Chicago *New-Church Independent*, where we find the "NEW Jerusalem" styled the worst "viper" and "harlot" in the Christian world (June 1888). But this hatred does not concern the absurd, fundamental dogmas of the sect, but its trinitarian priesthood (its "bishops", "pastors", and "priests").

The independents in the "New Jerusalem" correspond to the anti-popery criers in the "Old Jerusalem". The only students of Swedenborg, wholly independent of the anthropomorphic dogmas of the sect are the Buddhistic Swedenborgians. These are, however, strictly speaking not mere students of Swedenborg, but persons who, through the study of his writings have been lead to the study and acceptance of Buddhism. Many of them cooperate heartily in the work of the Theosophical Society.

In conclusion: It may be asked, Are all the members of the sect unaware of the patent, dual teaching of Swedenborg — content with looking at him through Mr. Hindmarsh's spectacles? Good reader, no more than all the members of the Church of England are content with looking at the New Testament through the Thirty-Nine Articles of Henry VIII.'s spectacles! The truth is that the foundations of the "New Jerusalem Church" are being sapped by its sceptics, freethinkers, and atheists — clerical and laical! Let us not insult the Brotherhood of Man by denying the presence of some little glimmer of that Ray of the Divine Sun — Reason — in any sect. I know that many members of the so-called "New Church" sigh for light to guide them out of the perplexities of Swedenborg's Christian theology; and to them and to all others I heartily recommend the Theosophical Society and its publications.

www.ingramcontent.com/pod-product-compliance
Lightning Source LLC
LaVergne TN
LVHW041503070426
835507LV00009B/783